Praise from those who know ...

★★★★★ An essential book for both authors and writers

Crowdfunding is the new way to raise money for your book project. Book Marketer Judith Briles knows the business. She has helped thousands of authors to publish. Get started on your book early by reading chapter 4: Timelines.

- Dan Poynter, the Father of Self-Publishing

★★★★★ What a gem

This handy little guide tells you just what you need to find your way through the book crowd-funding maze—not too much, not too little. I'm recommending this book to any author who wants to know about this timely topic. I doubt there's a better resource out there.

- Sandra Beckwith, Build Book Buzz

A Valuable Crowd Funding Resource

The audiobook's greatest strength is that it is densely packed; no filler. The book's greatest weakness is that it is densely packed; the slightest slip in maintaining attention or loss of understanding merits a stab at the rewind button.

Dr. Briles has an easy to listen to voice and delivery style. Her diction was authoritatively crisp, but pleasant. Experienced consumers of audiobooks know that they aren't likely to be narrated in one sitting. I found myself doing this repeatedly while taking handwritten notes. Having to do this may provide one a strong stimulus to acquire the print or e-book format to complement the audiobook.
 - Bill Johnson, Audiobook Producer/Narrator

★★★★★ A Must-Have Book for Authors and Writers!

Judith Briles presents all the steps for planning and implementing a successful crowdfunding game plan in each chapter. I found the information in "Timelines" and "Social Media Checklist" chapters invaluable, though the whole book shouldn't be missed! I highly recommend this book for authors and writers seeking a clear, concise and practical guide to crowdfunding.
 - Jo Ann Kairys, verified purchase

★★★★★ If you're looking to fund your book, this is a must read!

Wow. Loved it. Easy to read. Very impactful. An Aha on every other page. There's no sugar

coating in this book as Judith tells the reader upfront that "Crowdfunding is work" ... and to be successful, it is.
- Mitchell Levy, Chief Aha Instigator, Aha Amplifier

★★★★★ The crowdfunding "bible", a must-have resource for authors!

This is the crowdfunding "bible"—your most valuable resource as you start your next book project. Judith Briles' book is condensed enough not to overwhelm, complete enough to protect you from errors, and inspiring enough to convince you that it's time to get started. Don't miss owning this valuable resource!
- Mara Purl, *What the Heart Knows*, Amazon verified purchase

★★★★★ Invaluable Resource for CrowdFunding

Looking to learn about CrowdFunding and you are an author? This is the handy handbook that you need. It provides you guidance and tips for accomplishing your goals in an easy to read format.
- Amazon Customer

★★★★★ Its' a fact asking for money isn't easy, and getting it is even harder

Short—sweet and to the point. A must read for anyone considering a try at crowd funding.

- RBD, Amazon verified purchase

★★★★★ I wish I'd had this book before I ran my ...

I wish I'd had this book before I ran my first crowdfunding campaign. Judith Briles makes the essentials of crowdfunding clear and concise. This book really trims the fat off of the process of pitching your project: if you're just starting out, or even a seasoned campaigner. You need this book!

- Traee Dunblazier, Amazon verified purchase

★★★★★ The book on crowdfunding I recommend to authors

Judith Briles provides exactly the resource indie authors need to make their way through the crowdfunding jungle. From planning to platforms to real-world strategies, this is the go-to guide that I'll be recommending.

- Joel Friedlander, *A Self-Publisher's Companion*

How to Create Crowdfunding Success for Authors and Writers

Dr. Judith Briles
The Book Shepherd

Mile High Press, Ltd.
www.MileHighPress.com
MileHighPress@aol.com
303-885-2207

MileHigh Press

How to Create Crowdfunding Success for Authors and Writers
© 2022 Judith Briles
All rights reserved.
No part of this book may be reproduced in any written, electronic, recording, or photocopying form without written permission of the publisher. The exception would be in the case of brief quotations embodied in critical articles or reviews and pages where permission is specifically granted by the publisher.

Although every precaution has been taken to verify the accuracy of the information contained herein, the author and publisher assume no responsibility for any errors or omissions. No liability is assumed for damages that may result from the use of information contained within.

Books may be purchased in quantity
by contacting the publisher directly:
Mile High Press
8122 S Quatar Circle, Aurora CO 80016
303-885-4460

Editing: John Maling, EditingByJohn@aol.com
Interior Design: Nick Zelinger, NZGraphics.com
Cover and eBook Design: Rebecca Finkel, F+P Design
Illustrations: Don Sidle, www.DonSidle.com

ISBN: 978-1-885331-92-2 (Paper)
ISBN: 978-1-885331-93-9 (eBook)
ISBN: 978-1-885331-94-6 (Paper IngramSpark)
ISBN: 978-885331-99 (Audiobook)
LCCN: 2015938456

1. Publishing   2. Crowdfunding   3. Author   4. Business

Second Edition   Printed in the United States

CONTENTS

Author's Note 1

Just the Crowdfunding Facts, Dear Author ...
Just the Facts 5

1 Money Crunches and Author Overwhelm ... 13

2 Meet Some of the Key Players for
Authors to Do the Lifting 25

3 The Costs & Taxes 31

4 Timelines 37

    3 Months to 1 Year before
Your Crowdfunding Launch 38

    1 to 3 Months before
Your Crowdfunding Launch 41

    Zero Day to 1 Month before
Your Crowdfunding Launch 44

    During the Campaign 45

        Post Campaign Completion 47

5 Essentials for Crowdfunding
Success 49

    Your Pitch Video 52

    Written Pitch 53

    Small Campaign Image 54

    Rewards 55

Links 58
Record What's Happening 59
Online Chatter about You! 60
6 Social Media Checklist 63
7 Tips for Momentum and the Final Push ... 71
8 Updates 73
9 Creating a CrowdFunding GamePlan 75
10 One More Thing 81
BONUS! Crowdfunding Cheat Sheet 83
Thanks to My Village 89
Meet Judith Briles, The Book Shepherd 95
Working with Judith 1013

Author's Note

Imagine an eBay-type website for investing and donating, where you could login and browse causes and businesses, and find an "investment" or "cause" that appeals to you, even a book idea.

Imagine creating your own "spot" on that site where all those browsers can discover *you* ... and do a happy dance to see that your book project is exactly what they were looking to give some money to.

The moneys given could be as nominal as $5 or much larger, more than $1,000. The contributor becomes part of a community, and over time, sees the impact of his or her donation/investment. How cool is that?

How would you like to fund your book project using OPM ... other people's money ... and not have to pay it back? You can. Welcome to Crowdfunding.

Crowdfunding, at its essence, is exactly that—connecting "crowds" directly to those who need funds: we authors.

Crowdfunding websites offer a hassle-free way to find, vet, and support individuals, companies, causes and organizations, and contribute or invest directly without a middleman.

It's more personal and impactful—giving you direct access to information and opportunities that were once the exclusive domain of people "in the know." Today, many thousands of authors have funded their entire book project using OPM ... other people's money.

It's amazing how every $25 eventually adds up to many thousands ... the difference in getting your book done and in hands ... and not. It's important to do your homework—*to determine a realistic estimate of the cost of the project.*

Before you enthusiasticly say, "I'm all in," it's important to do a reality, *come-to-book talk with yourself*. **Crowdfunding is work**—don't kid yourself. Roughly 35 percent of publishing related campaigns succeed. That means that 65 percent don't. You have to do the work to pull it off. There's pre-work in the set up; work during the campaign at launch through the end of its timespan; and then there's post-work at fundraising completion.

Since inception through 2021, the primary crowdfunding sites that support publishing projects have generated over 17 billion dollars. There is money out there. Money that would be a fit for you and your vision. Do you want some of it? You have to have a Plan. You have to plan to do the ASK.

Here's the #1 secret to a crowdfunding book campaign: a good idea and hard work. If you believe in your book and are willing to put in the work ... read on!

Judith

P.S. Here's my ask ... after you've read, would you post a review on Amazon ... we authors are grateful when you support us in this way.

Just the Crowdfunding Facts, Dear Author ... Just the Facts

Crowdfunding is BIG business ... as in a mega billion dollar industry the seeds dreams and takes entrepreneurs to places they never imagined. Authors are authorpreneurs ... beginning businesses that need spirit, energy, commitment ... and money. Crowdfunding may be the resource to not only seed your publishing spirit, but to grow it.

There are zillions of crowdfunding stats. Below are several—Statista and Kickstarter are my resources in 2022 based on the previous year's data. In turn, they are pulled from the major crowdfunding sites as well. Kickstarter updates it's site regularly with data—you don't have to wait until year end to see how groups are doing. Some are general to give you the BIG picture; some are specific to publishing. Most likely, the ones that interest you the most.

It's essential to remember that crowdfunding success does not occur on a whim. It requires careful planning and strategizing. Your time will be a significant factor to its success. There were over 6 million projects in 2021 ... something that is projected double by the time 2023 ends.

- ✓ It's a billions industry magnet: over $17 billion was generated just in North America campaigns.
- ✓ Crowdfunding is expanding: up 33.7% from 2020.
- ✓ The world loves crowdfunding. Last year, there were 6,455,080 worldwide crowdfunding campaigns.
- ✓ The over-all AVERAGE success rate for all campaigns is 22.4%.

- ✓ The over-all AVERAGE success rate for publishing campaigns is 35% on Kickstarter.

- ✓ On average, *successful* campaigns have raised $28,656. This includes all categories that campaigns are identified with. Categories like and Comics are huge money gathers.

- ✓ On average, the average amount raised by all campaigns was less than $850. That means there are far more unsuccessful campaigns than successful.

- ✓ The more backers a campaign has, the higher the probability of success in reaching the campaign goal. Fully funded projects average 300; an average of all campaigns is 47.

- ✓ The average pledge for fully funded projects is just shy of $100: $96 per pledge.

- ✓ Videos are a must. You double the amount of funds committed for your campaign by having one. It's YOU talking to your donors through the camera eye.

- ✓ Let donors know who you are—your name and photo at least. Why? You can get 79% more backers.

- ✓ Successful crowdfunding campaigns that raise at least 30% of their goal within their first week are more likely to reach their goal. Momentum is needed from the get-go.

- ✓ eMail sharing is hot. When you promote via email and your recipient shares it with others in his or her circle, there is a 53% probability that a donation will be coming your way. Therefore: ask for the share with others and build your email list.

- ✓ Social media does create conversions to donations. Ranges vary from 3% (Twitter) to 12% (Facebook) … but a donation is a donation.

- ✓ The odds are in your favor if you're an AON campaign a la Kickstarter (All-or-Nothing) versus KIA (Keep-it-All) model campaigns. It's perceived that there's a higher success factor for completing a project if all the money is raised.

- ✓ Age matters. The under 45 group are more likely to support a campaign than the over

45. It means your reach out must have "lure" factors for all ages from 24 and up.

✓ Planning and strategizing are musts. The average is 11 days ... assuming you are not starting from a full scratch your head position. You have a video to create; content for the platform's campaign template; images to gather up; rewards to offer that will be compelling to the donor; eblasts and social media postings ... and more.

✓ Words count for the detail info page on your crowdfunding platform. Successful campaigns average 300 to 500 words. Get to the point. Your key pitch is upfront in the first paragraph. Always have a CTA—call to action at your close (this is in the video as well).

✓ Most campaigns range from 30 to 45 days once the campaign opens for donations. Successful campaigns talk the campaign up until the campaign is over. That means social media and eblasts. It also means communicating updates with those who have already committed. If you don't, you significantly increase the possibility of failure.

✓ Not only do updates allow you to earn more, but they will also likely determine whether your crowdfunding campaign reaches its goal in the first place. Campaigns that updated followers regularly raised 126% more than those with no updates. Kickstarter reported that posted updates increased overall success probabilities by 58.7%. With no updates, probability for success dropped to less than 33%.

✓ The first and last three days of an average crowdfunding campaign is where and when most of the money flows in—approximately 42%.

✓ Kickstarter has had the most completed projects of all the platforms.

✓ IndieGoGo projects have raised an average of $41,634 each—the highest average amount of any of the platforms.

Whew! That's a boatload of information to get your head around. But it's necessary to understand what you are walking into. The crowdfunding market is only going to get bigger. One reason is that the entrepreneur and even established small businesses are bypassing traditional financial resources for startup assistance: banks. By 2030, crowdfunding is projected to grow to $300 billion.

As I write this, the sweet spot for donations is under $100 each. Not a huge amount of money for someone who believes in what you are doing. Overall, 75% of campaigns seek less than $10,000 ... 100 x $100 = $10,000; 100 x $50 = $5,000.

It is about planning. It is about marketing. It is about promoting. It is about you and your ideas. You can do this!

Your book project will be doing the Author Happy Dance.

Money Crunches and Author Overwhelm

Let's face it, many of the costs to publish today can be overwhelming. When Crowdfunding surfaced as an option, authors were able for the first time to get total strangers to say with a "click"—"I like this idea and will donate money toward its completion."

Is it easy? Nope ... Can anyone do it? Yes ... in most cases. You need a GamePlan and a Crowdfunding Sherpa of some sort to get you started. Your Sherpa could be the video tutorial type, a written "how to" guide or a real person. You avoid mistakes this way ... mistakes that could ultimately cost you thousands of dollars and hundreds of hours to rectify.

> **The odds that you can raise the moneys you need are extremely high, with planning, focus and perseverance in your corner.**

It's a growing world, one that has seeded mega-millions of dollars in funding for literary projects globally. Crowdfunding is a tool where authors just might find the right crowd who will support their ideas and book in a combined social-networking-with-project-fundraising.

Well-known authors, like Seth Godin, have used Crowdfunding to seed and in some cases, finance their entire book projects (Godin raised $40,000 in less than four hours via *Kickstarter.com*). Disclaimer: He has a huge social media following; he's known as an out-of-the-box (actually change-the-box) thinker and doer; and his previous books have been significant bestsellers. The odds that you will raise what he did in a few hours are extremely remote. BUT, the odds that you *can* raise the moneys you *need* are extremely high, with planning, focus and perseverance in your corner.

In the Beginning

It always starts with an idea, and then the rest is up to you. What are you pitching to your fans, your crowd, your soon-to-be fans and crowd? What are you going to "gift" them if they send $10, $25, $50, $100, $500, $1000 or more (let's think big!)—people like perks.

What are you going to give these awesome supporters? A postcard with your name on it? A book? An eBook? Invitation to lunch? Private webinar just for contributors? Their names in the book? Their names as characters in the book? Their street (or city or place of business) named in the book? What?

Charles Fischer's goal was to raise $7,800—he overfunded his debut YA book, *Beyond Infinity*, for $8,300 plus. Offering a variety of rewards

to supporters, he tapped into
his talents for a big one—he
offered a "customized
workshop that focused on
writing for either students
or adults." Charles had one
taker at $1,000. You can
view Charles' funded
campaign here:

http://tinyurl.com/BeyondInfinityBook.

Ashlee Bratton is a professional photographer.
Her goal was to raise $8,500 for her book project,
Life Before the Lottery: The 30 x 30 List.
She succeeded in overfunding
her project with $9,635 raised
when her thirty day campaign
was over. Her rewards to
donors ranged from a
"sassy motivation postcard"
for $10 to a "professional
portrait sitting that included an
overnight stay in a B&B" for $1,500—one taker
jumped at that; two others nabbed her $1,000
offer. What Ashlee did was tap into her skills
and put a dollar sign with them. Obviously,

supporters agreed. You can view Ashlee's funded campaign here: *http://tinyurl.com/LifeBeforeTheLottery.*

Dianne Maroney had a dream—it became *The Imagine Project* and 154 backers shared it with her, bringing in $22,394. To encourage her backers, she offered everything from a "hearty thank you" for $1; a "down-loadable song created for the project" at $5; a "limited edition, ready to frame, 8 x 10 signed print from the project, along with three signed copies of the book and listing your name in the appreciation page" for $250. You can view Dianne's funded campaign here: *http://tinyurl.com/TheImagineProjectBook.*

Expect most contributions to be under $100. The average project seeks $5,000 with a wide range from $500 to mega-thousands. Be realistic, then set your goal and go for it! What's interesting, more like amazing, is that some will contribute to your cause—the book—just because they like the sound of it or what you are doing.

Once you lay out your presentation on why YOU, why your BOOK and all the other marvelous REWARDS ... rewards you will offer that come to each donor on the funding website you partner with (meaning you will pay some type of fundraising fee) ... it then goes out to the cyber universe. Savvy authors include a video—stats show that it increases moneys raised by 100 percent plus! YOU, of course, should be letting everyone and their uncle know about the BOOK and the project and the link to go to. Where do you go to learn more (and create your own project)? There's a variety of sites, and surely more to come.

The major sites you should consider for your campaign are: *KickStarter.com* (exceeding six billion dollars in total funded projects through 2021); Go Fund Me (raising over 9 billion since its 2010 inception).

Kickstarter.com does a huge number of books ... but again, there is a BUT—it does not support "causes" or a charity. It's the gorilla in the playground and has funded more than $200 million for literary projects.

Caution: Kickstarter can be picky. Groucho Marx said he would never join a club that would have him as a member. Groucho would have had a much easier time getting into IndieGoGo and GoFundMe. They take almost everybody. Keep that in mind.

4 Critical Questions You Must Ask Yourself

1. *Is my project worth it?*

Really ... is it worth it? Be honest. Is this an ego thing ... or is your story, your how-to/solution new with a twist? Does it have a WOW to it? Is it interesting? If you can't honestly say yes, yes, yes and yes, the odds are that you are going to struggle with getting funding. If people—your family and friends included—can't get excited, do you expect perfect strangers to?

2. *Is my book concept compelling?*

You have your hat in hand ... you are asking for money. Okay, what's going to "seduce" the donor? What's the aha ... what's the benefit for the completed book to the reader ... what will the donor get in return—yes, feeling good in supporting you ... but is there anything else? Having great rewards count here as well. People will want to know how you will use their money; what they will get in return; and yes, that you are a good steward in moving the project forward. The video that you make must include this.

3. *Do I think that my Crowdfunding project will fund itself?*

Think again. If you do, you set yourself up for instant failure. In 2021, Kickstarter reported statistics that the overall success rate of all its Crowdfunding projects was just under 40 percent. In the publishing category, 56,170 were started. In dollars, the successful projects raised $213 million with a success rate of 35 percent.

Don't be disillusioned—just because Kickstarter is where massive traffic is doesn't necessarily mean that's where you should be with your book project. Big crowds doesn't mean that you or your book will attract them—and don't ever get caught up in the denial, and I mean denial, that a few Tweets and Facebook postings will do for you. You want to amplify what you are doing. By the time you are finished, there will be many hundreds of postings scattered among your main social media platforms.

You have a campaign to run—and it needs your full attention pushing through each of the days. Your marketing (yes, that is exactly what you are doing) needs to be far-reaching, ongoing and, gulp, effective for you to succeed.
I view your crowdfunding campaign as a "pre-launch" of the book. It sets the stage for building book buzz.

4. *Are my rewards appropriate and alluring ... or are they mundane?*

First, have at least seven in the mix. Many backers support you solely on what your book is about, while others look for goodies— those rewards that come to them, depending on how much they commit to. Creativity counts and those rewards should relate to the level of financial commitment.

As an ace author/photographer, when Ashlee Bratton offered a full photo shoot at a beautiful bed and breakfast site that included two nights lodging—of course this wasn't for a $50 commitment, it went for $1,500. Among your rewards may be eBooks, autographed printed books, may be book club chats, private workshops, teas (romance authors do well with this). Explore what others are doing ... and then ask yourself, *Do any of these work for my book project? or What can I offer to my supporters with a twist?*

Don't reinvent the money wheel-study what others have done to be successful in crowdfunding.

Meet Some of the Key Players for Authors to Do the Lifting

When crowdfunding is in your midst, you have homework. Explore the websites of the platforms you are considering. Look at past successful publishing campaigns. Pay attention to the opening (video); rewards—how they are presented and which got them most traction; and how the author did the "ask" for support.

KICKSTARTER

Kickstarter is an all or nothing process. If you do not reach your preset funding goal, you do not get to keep any of the money pledged, whether you earned a nickel or fell one dollar short (the wise author gets out his credit card and completes the funding—you don't want to start over). There is no flexibility.

Kickstarter has only one way—its way—to raise moneys, and it can be picky with who it allows to use its portal. IndieGoGo, and Upspringer offer flexibility.

And, if your project is charity or cause-based, it will be rejected by Kickstarter.

> You want to mirror successful projects in your planning strategy.

IndieGoGo offers BOTH the all or nothing—the *fixed funding plan* as well as a *flexible* option—where you keep what you earned minus the fees. If you go with the flexible option and don't meet your goal, the fees are more than 12 percent, which is the highest in the industry.

GoFundMe is for anyone who desires to raise money for what they are passionate about. If your book project is related to a cause, this may be your spot.

Each of the sites has tutorials. Watch the campaigns that have succeeded. Study them. They will also identify projects that have recently been completed. Learn from them—how they present in general and their variety of rewards. Since IndieGoGo and Kickstarter do a variety of projects, narrow yours first to the category *publishing*. Kickstarter keeps past campaigns available on their websites for an indefinite period of time. Kickstarter is all about books, so all its completed projects will evolve around books and publishing.

All the sites shout out their successes. Read away. Look at their videos and content. What was the amount set for the goal? How many days were in the campaign? What was shown in the video? What was said? How long was it? Was there a call to action? What's in the promotional text on the project page? What's there to convince people to pledge money? How are the rewards that are being offered for contributions structured? How many rewards are there?

Pretend that you are a potential supporter of the project—what grabs you about the info as it's presented in text. What doesn't? What about the video—again, what works, what doesn't? How were the gifts/rewards presented? Was there anything unique about the presentation and the display of the funding page?

You want to mirror successful projects. Was it just the theme? Or was it something that the author did to get potential donors to buy in? Instead of reinventing the money wheel, study what others have done to be successful and pull nuggets from their success for your own campaign.

Free money has a cost-your cost will range from 10 to 20 percent of total funds sought: funding platform fees, credit card processing fees and rewards to donors.

The Costs & Taxes

Is *there a cost?* Yes there is. Nothing is free, really. Expect to fork over anywhere from 7 to 20 percent of what you raise. Sites like IndieGoGo pay a percentage back if you meet your goal within the time you set. It also releases whatever you raise at the end of the campaign on the flexible side and does state so up front to all donors. Kickstarter requires that you raise all moneys—there is no flexible side—otherwise, the campaign is deemed unsuccessful. Most release your moneys once the campaign is completed successfully.

Note: I've worked with several platforms. There are pros and cons of each. It it's essential to have the opportunity of lots of eyes on your campaign that you didn't personally drive to it via emails and social media, Kickstarter delivers the best window.

What does each company take for its services? It's not free. Kickstarter's fee system is much simpler to explain. It takes 5 percent. It takes an additional 3-5 percent, depending on whether you are paying via your bank, domestic credit card or international credit card.

IndieGoGo has a tiered payment plan. Under the *fixed funding plan*, IndieGoGo takes a 4 percent fee, plus 3 percent for credit card payment, for a total of 7 percent. If you choose its flexible funding plan, which allows you to keep whatever amount you raised but you DON'T hit your goal, IndieGoGo takes 9 percent + 3 percent (credit card) for a total of 12 percent. If you reach the goal, the total take is the 7 percent as laid out above. GoFundMe changes 2.9% plus .30 per donation.

Plans, of course, are subject to change so make sure you check what the latest rates are before you dive in.

> **The tax man does cometh. Declare all moneys you bring in on your taxes. Crowdfunding is one "gift" that is taxable to you.**

Rewards Costs ... don't leave this off the table. When someone gives you $50, you will offer "something" in return. It could be a printed book, an eBook or something else. There is a cost—actual cost, a shipping cost or someone getting it to the person who has earned it. There is a cost. It's part of your budget. The savvy author-to-be will budget in a 5-7 percent cost.

If you think that $10,000 will cover the manufacturing costs of your book—editing, cover design, layout, printing—you need to add in the cost of the campaign platform PLUS the cost of rewards. Maybe the real cost is closer to $11,500 with $1,500 toward rewards and campaign costs.

This is a budget item—just be aware of it upfront.

Taxes

Don't play games and assume that since the moneys were a gift, it's not taxable. If you are in the United States, declare all moneys received on your tax returns the year you receive them—most likely you will have plenty of offset expenses. For other countries, do what is appropriate within your country.

Keep good records of all your expenses as well as the income—they will offset much of what you receive. And, if you know that you will have expenses the next year—i.e., layout or editing, you can certainly pre-pay them so you have it out of the way and it will be a legitimate expense for tax purposes.

And note to self … if you expect to show a profit, put some of your proceeds away to pay your tax bill.

Family and friends create the cornerstone of your campaign. They need to be first out of the donor sign-up gate.

Timelines

Planning is critical for your success. Once you decide that you are going to do a crowdfunding campaign, the clock begins to tick.

Pre-Launch

Your timeline can be a few weeks to many months out before your official launch. The few weeks means that you have critical essentials in place, mainly social media and your family/friends know what's coming. Outside of an outright financial gift with no strings attached, winning a mini-lottery or happening upon a wad of cash out of the blue, where else are you going to get thousands of dollars that doesn't come from your own pocket that could fund you book? There's work to be done.

> **Family and friends are at the core of every funded campaign.**

3 Months to 1 Year before Your Crowdfunding Launch

This is the time you start your list building. It's your gold mine. Names and emails are what you are after. If you are young, include the friends of your parents and other over-40 adults in your family. Why—simply this: the average donor is in the 40 to 50 age range with a large number in their early 40s. What parent and friend of a parent doesn't like to boast about what their young adult kids are doing to make their way in the world?

Funded campaigns have a common core—the family and friend factor. You are doing a quick head count to make sure that there will be a financial commitment of support, as in 30 percent of total moneys sought. If you are seeking $5,000—you want to know that you can count on $ 1,500 coming from this group from the get-go when you go live; if $10,000—it's $3,000. The more, the better.

List building isn't something you do in an hour. You may put together some names quickly—but it's all the add-ons that will build your base. It takes time and you will quickly discover it's a multiplying factor. *Who do you know who ...?* Who do your friends know who might be interested in your book idea ... or even in you?

- ✓ *Social Media, Social Media, Social Media.* Start following and building back. Twitter and Facebook will be key. Dig down into your genre area and discover "like"—each of the platforms have companion sites and tools that have been created to assist you in building. Start early.

- ✓ *Friends and Relatives ... start list building.* Yes, you know your family; and yes, you know who your friends are. Let them know what you are up to. Who would support you and guestimate what amounts you could receive. This group is elementary to your success. It's all you know—those you share greetings with, birthday cards with, send out a birth announcement with, any type of holiday greeting with, thinking of you with, etc. Then go through it and do some weeding—not all will be a fit.

✓ *Colleagues and Coworkers ... the list continues.* And continues. A crowdfunding campaign isn't the time to be shy, withdrawn and remote. Gather names and emails of potential contacts to alert them when the formal launch begins.

✓ *Friends of Friends.* Ask your friends if they have friends that might be interested in what you are doing. Ideally, your friends will contact their friends and encourage them to join the party.

✓ *Friends Who Have Social Media Tribes.* Who is "wired" in your circle? If they love what you are doing, why not tell all their followers? Why not, indeed. Some will offer to join in when the campaign officially opens and encourage their contacts to support your Crowdfunding campaign. Ask them if they will.

✓ *On your "To Do" List will be Create Tweets and Postings for Others.* Yes, indeed—not only will you share the big launch with all, you will create a few Tweets and other postings that you will send out a few days before the BIG launch to all on your list and ask them to tell their friends-followers-fans what's happening. All they need to do is copy, paste and send out. Make it easy to support you.

1 to 3 Months before Your Crowdfunding Launch

✓ *eMail Gathering Continues.* Don't be surprised when people will say they are interested and want to be contacted when your launch begins—then vanish. It happens. There will be a percentage that come through; many won't.

✓ *Book Cover and Support Branding.* Having your book cover (even if it changes during the evolution post-funding) delivers a visual of what's to come.

- ✓ *Create Content for Crowdfunding Platform.* Video, text for pages, gather images to include.

- ✓ *Crowdfunding Platform Site.* You are building a landing page for your project that has a variety of elements to it. The good news is that you don't have to "think up" what you need—you will get a step-by-step guide with the platform you choose to build your campaign on. What you need is to supply the content that goes in each. Think snap, crackle and pop in presentation. You want this completed several weeks before launch day.

- ✓ *Build Rewards.* Study what other successful campaigns have presented for rewards— what types appeared to be the most successful (you will tell this by the greatest number taken)? Create descriptions. Add a few that are "back-ups" to be used as a substitute for one that is posted and not being subscribed to or as a Bonus at the end of the campaign to lure already committed supporters into contributing a second round of funding.

✓ *Make your Video.* When your campaign starts, consider adding an additional video—updating your supporters of any news. You can have a professional do it or DIY. What it needs is the heartfelt outreach, the why you are doing it, what the benefit will be to the reader, what you are doing with the moneys, and a call to action.

✓ *Refine your Marketing Strategy.* Many authors automatically go to Kickstarter because it's huge and they think because of size, the sheer volume of traffic it gets will automatically bring donors to them. Wrong thinking. Because of its size, you can be lost easily.

Will you get looky-loos wherever you launch from? Sure. But the real success will come from your own push—your friends and relatives and the list building you did prior to launch.

> **Stay focused ... you will need to say "NO" to a lot of things you normally do during your campaign. Don't do well what you have no business doing.**

Zero Launch Day to 1 Month before Your Crowdfunding Launch

✓ *Crowdfunding Platform Site* – if you haven't loaded your content, get this completed pronto. It's time to review with a sharp eye:

1 - Does it look good?

2 - Do images and any videos load quickly?

3 - Is your video engaging? Are you sharing why you are seeking moneys and what they will be used for? Do you have a call to action to the viewer?

4 - Are your rewards enticing and "feel" right for the amount levels you are seeking?

5 - Video updates. Watch what you have created. Ask those who are supporters to do the same.

6 - After viewing all videos and reading all content, would *you* support your campaign if you were a stranger?

7 - Share your site link with those you trust and ask the above six questions.

- ✓ *eMail Updates.* Send out an email to all that your Crowdfunding Launch is a week away—you are excited. Think of it is a "short" update, you aren't asking for moneys directly ... yet.

- ✓ *Social Media.* Update all your postings samples and send to your "inner circle"—all those on your list who have agreed to share with their friends and followers a week before you push out.

- ✓ *Create Press Release.* Yes—create an official shout out about what you are doing and release this within two weeks of your debut. Send to local media as well as free posting sites like *PressReleasePing.com*.

During the Campaign

Focus. Focus. Focus. My personal Keepers here are: *If you never say NO, your YESES become worthless* and *Don't do well what you have no business doing.* Being myopic is a good thing. For this month, you will live and breathe your campaign. That's it. You aren't going on a vacation, traveling, deciding to write a new book or start a new hobby/project ... no, your primary work is managing and completing your campaign.

- ✓ Keep growing your network – the more, the merrier.
- ✓ Launch email campaign and social media – the clock is running.
- ✓ Push your press release out – share with the media what you are doing … and if your campaign hits funding early, that's a valid *TaDah … Local Author Overfunds Crowdfunding for Next Book!*
- ✓ Post updates – on your personal social media of what's happening.
- ✓ Make a new video – use it to highlight the status of what's happening and/or something that is newsy about the book or you and post on campaign page and all your social media.
- ✓ Thank supporters – as they come in.
- ✓ Tweak rewards – if one doesn't have takers, pull it and substitute another.
- ✓ Tweak emails – plan on sending a once weekly update during the month outside of the emails used to promo the campaign.

✓ Send updates to supporters – at least on a weekly basis.

Post Campaign Completion

✓ Announce your results to all supporters.

✓ Thank everyone. Send directly to your contributors and publicly announce successful completion and thank your supporters as a group (you won't be naming them individually).

✓ Do a press release announcing your success and seed what the book is about and when available (don't use a firm date—i.e., Summer 2022 gives you a three month window from the third week in June to the third week in September).

✓ Get your rewards out as promised.

Celebrate your success!
You get to choose your Reward!

Crowdfunding success is like a classic recipe-learn and use the essential ingredients and the outcome will be a perfect book dish.

Essentials for Crowdfunding Success

- *Video*—(less than two minutes pitching project ... make sure you say what you are doing with the money—most don't).

- *Content*—what the story/book is about.

- *Bio*—it's your show time ... why you are the one to write this book.

- *Photos or illustrated images*—add to the excitement and visual display of campaign page.

- *Rewards*—your donors like supporting the project and they love the rewards as well ... see what others offer and start with that as a model.

- *Family/Friends*—people want to see legs starting on a campaign. Ask/plead/tell family and friends to step up to the plate once you hit the 25-30 percent mark, others start climbing on board. You want family and friends to sign on within the first few days of the campaign.

- *Set time limit*—30 to 45 days are the most successful.

- *Communicate*—update your supporters on what's going on. Don't be shy; you may need to ask for more. And go back to your own circles of contacts more than once.

- *Social media*—you will shout out everywhere that you have a campaign going. Campaigns are not successful without this—the exception would be that you have such a massive email list that all you have to do is contact them and say, "Go-Go-Go," and they do it. Otherwise, you will ask your fans, friends and followers for their support and to do shout outs to those who they are connected with. And you will do it often.

- *Image*—this instantly identifies your campaign brand and is clickable.

- *Links*—you want to have live links to your campaign on all your social media sites as well as your personal and business websites.

- *Book Cover*—if you have yours, even if it evolves, images carry weight. Consider this a pre-investment to the book—the sooner, the better.

Your Pitch Video

- Make a short video (no more than TWO minutes) that expresses you goals and intentions. It's your story—you have a window to get your audience to catch your vision and join the journey.

- A video is a critical component of your campaign and an absolute must—don't skip doing one.

- You are the star in it—make it personal, heartfelt, never arrogant. And talk to the camera.

- Give contributors a sneak peek of your book project and what you are going to be doing with the moneys.

- Humor is fun—even a hint of silliness. Be you and allow some of your personality to flow—leaving a smile on your donors' faces, a feeling that they are delighted to have discovered you.

- Consider using music—helps sets a tone for the video and the campaign. Critical: Secure written releases for any copyrighted material.

- Make sure the video is clear and concise—use visuals and make sure it's audible.

- Call out the spirit of collaboration. You're not just asking for moneys, you're inviting people to help you work on something to share with others.

- End with a clear call to action—don't leave them hanging.

Written Pitch

- Put the most important information first.

- Tell a story—but don't make it too long (consider time and attention spans).

- Explain exactly why you are fundraising.

- Tell the viewer a bit about yourself and those who are involved with your book.

- Build trust with a breakdown of your budget—they want to know where the money is going.

- Spelling and grammar are important. Proofread!

- Break long text into sections with headings and images.

- Make it visual—include images in your pitch.

A great pitch is like a one to two sentence blurb you would find for a hot movie coming up. Designed to grab the viewer at once.

Small Campaign Image

- Make sure your image is relevant to your campaign and visually interesting!

- This is your campaign's most visible image—people should be compelled to click on it to become the newest member of your community.

- Your image stands as your campaign brand.

Rewards

- Make reward names and descriptions clear.
- Consider the value of each—make sure you can fulfill all rewards and still complete your project.

- Offer a broad range of rewards—from $10 thank yous on your website to $1,000+ something that offers unique experiences. By the way—those $10 spots help your book campaign to go viral—the more you have, the more cyber attention you get.

- Call out the urgency of a reward availability related to the length of your campaign. Use words like "limited edition", "exclusive" and "early-bird."

- Create rewards that will connect the contributor to the project **emotionally** as well as physically.

- Consider your reward strategy—offer a $50 perk and a $100 perk ... 60 percent of your supporters will fall between these amounts.

- Be reasonable with your reward prices. Offering a T-shirt for $500 or a mug and pen for $1,000 isn't going to cut it with your possible contributors. Emotion is the driving force—appeal to it. Consider limiting anything you have to mail to go out to those who contribute more than $50 (that means an eBook goes to the under $50 crowd where a print book is over).

- Be creative! T-shirts and stickers are inexpensive. Anything that requires a digital download is too. You may have (or can do) videos for a how-to book; a Skype or phone call; a gathering for a book club.

- If you are running a flexible funding campaign, keep in mind reward fulfillment in the event that you don't hit your goal. Kickstarter doesn't do flexible—IndieGoGo and GoFundMe do.

- Add pictures of your rewards in the pitch text (at least a few)! It adds personality and breaks up lots of text.

- You are usually limited to a maximum number of rewards at a time—if no one "bites" on one or some are "sold out," you can hide them and add others.

- You want your rewards easy and affordable to deliver. Expect the cost to range from five to seven percent to deliver (production, time, postage, etc.).

- $25, $50 and $100 are statistically the biggest sellers.

- Flatlines happen. Have something to jumpstart the "tired" phase of a campaign—it happens. When you hit a slump, what are you going to do? Think about a "hot" new reward that you've held back on—some kind of a special giveaway to anyone who has already given.

- Backup Rewards. Yes, create extra Rewards to offer to those who make additional contributions or to sub in one that isn't attracting takers.

Links

A must do: have live links to connect those you are shouting out to back to your campaign page PLUS re-sharing with all the main social media sites. And ...

- Add links to Facebook, Twitter, LinkedIn, Instagram, Pinterest and other social media related to your campaign.

- Add links to your business and personal websites—lots of outside links help legitimize your campaign—the more, the better. Don't forget to include Hashtags.

- Include a link to your campaign on your profile pages.

Record What's Happening

 Use **Instagram** to post pictures as your campaign builds momentum and tell your social media world—send emails to friends and supporters (take pictures of you creating your rewards or even just hanging out with your team).

- Take screen shots as campaign progresses and photos of any everts related to your project.

- Show pics of those who are involved with the book creation/production.

- Tag words that relate to your project and/or Crowdfunding efforts.

- Tag all pictures with a link to your campaign.
- Show people your perks, sneak peeks into your campaign, etc., with pictures.

Online Chatter about You!

Record it! Most computers come with screenshot capabilities. Use it. Not only share via Instagram ... blast news out on Twitter, Facebook, and Pinterest! With the image that you snag, show the numbers increasing, a pic of your "hot" reward taken via your screen. Use your imagination. Amplify you and your project everywhere you can.

**The Internet is the
Money Town Hall for
your crowdfunding success.
The more you are connected
with it, the greater the
probability is for reaching
your financial goal.**

6

Social Media Checklist

Judith Briles, The Book Shepherd

Your Tweets, Facebook postings, Blogs and other social media portals are critical to your success. Social media is a communications tool, not a media outlet. Communications are two-way—that means you need to follow what you post. If others make comments, respond back. You need to be building your numbers. Not just a few hundred—you are looking for thousands. The more, the better. Friends that you know that have big Twitter and Facebook connections can be extremely helpful when you launch your campaign. They can do shout outs on your behalf to their followers to support your campaign.

- Identify active Bloggers, Twitterers and Facebookers who can help spread the word in your book's topic. Do a Google search with top influencers on Twitter in ___; top influencers on Facebook in ___; top bloggers in ___. Now connect and follow; add to the dialogue ... and you do this before you ever launch.

- Identify where the press release could be sent, and to whom at that magazine, blog, program (Wired, PR news release, NPR, university radio, etc.).

- Ask yourself and friends: Are there any celebs (major and minor) active on social media who might take an interest in your theme or topic? Do a Google search and ask the same thing.

- Draft postings—Tweets, Posts for Facebook. LinkedIn and Instagram with link to your campaign asking for help. If you don't ask, you won't get—always keep that in mind.

Get ready to be your own publicist. Anything is possible when it comes to news—getting others to blog about you is always a plus.

For Twitter ...

- Use popular and trending hashtags to raise awareness for your campaign.

- Always, always, always include your campaign link whenever you are tweeting about it.

- Ask for Retweets to help spread the word—write "please Retweet" with each Tweet.

- Tweet at people (even those you don't know) who might have a special interest in the subject of your campaign.

- Gain followers by following others and actively engaging them.

- Don't OD your Twitter stream.

- Create a "master list" of Tweets and ask your inner circle to Tweet them out throughout the campaign to their followers.

- Tell all your Follower Peeps about your rewards—be specific!

- Tweets that are snappy, sassy and sometimes salty get the followers!

For Facebook ...

- Use both your personal Facebook and a Facebook page for the campaign to send regular updates on your campaign.

- Always include a link to your campaign whenever you are writing about it on Facebook.

- Ask people for feedback and engage them with questions.

- People are more likely to "Like" and "Share" media! Show people your perks, sneak peeks into your campaign, etc., with pictures and videos.

- Tell people about your perks—be specific!

Social media is a tool to communicate. That means you need to follow and respond when chatter is about you and/or your book. Think of it as a Town Hall.

For LinkedIn ...

- Send out regular updates on your campaign. Best time is before 8 a.m.

- Always include a link to your campaign whenever you are writing about it on LinkedIn.

- Ask people for feedback and engage them with questions.

- Tell people about your perks—be specific!

For Instagram

- Always include a link to your campaign whenever you are writing about it on Instagram.

- Use both your profile page and a business page if you have one (most use the profile page for posting. Send regular updates on your campaign.

- Show people your perks, sneak peeks into your campaign, etc., with pictures and videos. People are more likely to reshare and push it out to their followers.

- Instagram is all about images—take pictures of everything: rewards, progress ... everything.

- Show people your perks—be specific!

For Pinterest ...

- Use your Pinterest account to build your project's vision and "brand."

- Pin pictures of your rewards and anything else visually interesting relating to your project.

- Follow other "pinners" in the industry in order to receive a following for your campaign.

- Pin videos and images that lead back to your campaign.

Online Publicity ...

- Create a press release and distribute. Sites like *PRLog.com* and *PR.com* have a free feature and spreads out nationally. Identify all possible forums, blogs, and news site to send press release to and could post in comments—or get people to post blogs about.

- Don't forget your local press. Yes, the print community in newspapers is evaporating. What is alive is the local community—the throw-aways that look for space. Usually referred to as the "local weekly." Just Google "local weeklies" in your city and state as well ... you will be amazed at what pops up.

In my hometown of Denver, Colorado, we have *YourHub*—a printing once a week and online via the *Denver Post* that carries all the local happenings. A freebie, all one has to do is copy and paste and click submit. You never know what will be carried, but it's worth a try.

Tips for Momentum and the Final Push

Add *New rewards* throughout your campaign—the Crowdfunding groups have shown that more than 20 percent of repeat contributions (meaning they contributed once and are now adding to the original amount) are for rewards that were added after the campaign went live.

Create a referral Contest ... anyone who refers the most contributors to your campaign gets a prize. Make it "hot"!

Almost to the goal ... make sure you have an angel in your pocket. Campaigns are tiring and do lose steam. Have someone who will step in to complete the funding if you are within 15 percent of your goal—yes, you pay them back as soon as moneys come your way (usually within 30 days). It's crazy to get that far and lose out because you are $1,000 short.

Updates

Post about progress. Post about perks. Post about new perks. Post about a contest. Post your weekly percentage updates. Just post ... once or twice a week during the campaign. Campaigns tend to drag at the half-way mark. That's when you need your dancing shoes to engage your followers. Updates are a way to keep them interested—especially as you get to deadline and your financial goal. They want you to make it! And don't forget ... you need to ask for their support, their moneys. Updates on your Crowdfunding site are automatically sent to everyone who has contributed to or favorited your campaign. Your followers already like you ... hang in there!

Crowdfunding ... using other people's moneys to seed; to fund a type of pre-launch; to produce; to market to *do what?* with a new book. It is money from heaven for authors and writers who may not have the necessary personal funds to underwrite what is needed; who want to build buzz to get support; who are curious about this new way to bankroll a venture.

Creating a CrowdFunding GamePlan

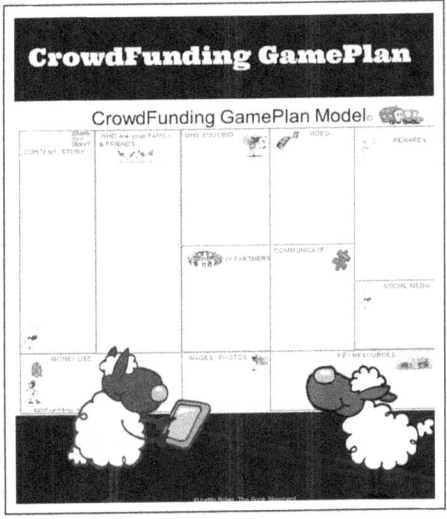

I'm a visual and like to have "it" all in front of me when I'm working on a project, which includes anything with my books—whatever "it" is. In creating *GamePlan Models© for Book Marketing, Writing the Book* and now *CrowdFunding*, I've found that it helps me get focused and stay focused. When I'm focused, I finish; when I'm not … I don't. I bet you are the same way.

The CrowdFunding GamePlan Model© for any project kick starts the organization for the team needed. It reminds me who I'm reaching out to seek support from, what kinds of rewards I need to offer and much more.

In my Unplugged events (*Book Publishing, Book Marketing, Social Media, Speaking, Amazon Bestseller, Podcast Super Guest*), participants actually get giant wall copies of the model to work on that are taped on the meeting room walls—when an idea hits, they can move to the walls and post on it. When the event is over, participants roll them up and take them home—a helpful visual to remind them "DO THIS" versus the typical notes getting buried in a notebook or file never to be seen again.

I use a variety of colored sticky notes and different colored markers ... I even draw or glue images to goose me toward the end. Sometimes I add a favorite quote, even a reminder to not do something. I might add a visual "reward" just for me when I reach my goal.

Your sections will include:

What's Your Story? What's so compelling that people—family, friends, total strangers—will want to get on board and say, "You bet, here's my money ... I believe in you, your book, your message ..."

Who are your Family and Friends? To be successful, family and friends are critical—as in 30 percent of all the total moneys you want to raise. Who are they and how much do you think they will commit to? The #1 mistake authors make is not having the financial support from their immediate circle.

Why You? You are the star here ... what's so hot about you? Is it your expertise, your passions, your commitment, your vision, your solutions, your insights, your what? People want to know. Do you have a Video? Lights, camera, action ... a critical component to every campaign is a short video (less than two minutes)—the shorter the better.

This is just for the project, nothing else. You can do a DIY with your phone; you can prop up a video camera and start talking; you can have props; you can have someone do it for you ... but you must do it. Consider making a few of them—as a backup to add if the one you initially post doesn't become the grabber you had hoped for

... or to add to the campaign as the days progress—share an update. The video can be serious, fun, even quirky. Just do it.

Don't forget to include a Call for Action ... in your video and in your written text on your landing page. Tell your viewers what you want them to do: participate by contributing moneys.

What Rewards will you offer? Offering goodies to supporters is what they want and expect. Be creative with whatever prizes and rewards you give at your donation levels.

How and when will you Communicate? Think Pre, During and Post the crowdfunding campaign, especially if the moneys you are seeking are for a book project that isn't completed. Donors don't want to be left in limbo—they want to know what you are doing; how you are doing. After all, they are now part of your team.

Where are you on Social Media? Social media and SEO (search engine optimization) are essential to your success. Using key words and phrases as you blast out to the cyber world in posts, Tweets and images that your project is in play are critical. You want to be found. Pronto.

Your social media presence will be fueled on an ongoing basis throughout the crowdfunding timeframe. You need a following—lots and lots of followers, friends and fans. Starting building—the #2 mistake authors make is not having a large social media following.

Do you have JV Partners? In addition to your own social media community, having partners who will shout out for you could be the difference between your success and failure—the failure side where 70 percent of publishing crowdfunding projects end up. Having them shout out to their fans, friends and followers that you are HOT and to support you is what you want them to say.

What will you do with the Moneys? It's always important. Potential supporters want to know what the moneys will be used for. Tell them. Do you have Images | Photos? What are you going to include in the content section of the crowdfunding platform you use? Do you need photos or special images created. Who will do it?

Who are your Key Resources? Who do you need on your team to pull this off? Virtual assistants; friends with plenty of social media contacts; an editor to make sure your copy content is crisp and has a strong call to action; help in dealing with the rewards that need to get out; who?

One More Thing

Even if you aren't using a specific crowdfunding platform, it doesn't mean that you shouldn't pay attention to other crowdfunding platforms' successfully funded projects. Subscribe to their blogs as well. Within each you will get *ahas'* on what's working, strategies, even gimmick ideas that just may be the cool thing to include in yours.

Be ready to lose some sleep—you will be tweaking your reach-outs and social media as you go along daily.

Here's to your awesome and successful campaign!

Crowdfunding is the authors and writers magic wand today.

CrowdFunding Cheat Sheet

12 Tips for Running a Successful Crowdfunding Campaign

1. **Don't rush into your campaign—Plan, Plan, Plan.**
   Successful crowdfunding campaigns require planning—from amount of moneys you'll need to what your costs will be.
2. **Learn the rules and how to play the game.**
   Each crowdfunding site has its own rules. Most must haves/dos are within the FAQs on their websites.

3. **Study and learn from other campaigns.**
   All the sites shout out about their successes. Narrow your search field to *publishing* (you must with Kickstarter, IndieGoGo, and GoFundMe)) and read away. Look at their videos and content. What was the amount set for the goal? How many days in the campaign? What was shown in the video? What was said? How long was it? Was there a call to action? What's on the promotional text on the project page? What's there to convince people to pledge moneys? How are the rewards that are being offered for contributions structured? How many rewards are there? What about images?

4. **Timing—long campaigns don't work.**
   Most campaigns are 30 days ... some go to 40. After that, it becomes a limp along affair. Your friends and family are first to the plate—most others wait until the tail end—don't prolong it. Many wait until the last minute to act, unless there is a special incentive to act early.

5. **Put a lot of thought and research into your funding goal.**

Your campaign costs will most likely run between 7 to 20 percent in fees connected to credit card and percentage of the campaign platform. Then there are your reward costs—you will need to determine full costs so you know what your net takeaway will be. Moneys received are taxable—you will have plenty of expenses to reduce the amount.

6   **Be Pitch perfect ...**
    in your video, in your text on the campaign page and in your social media.

7   **Have a video.**
    No exceptions—it tells your story, shows you as a person, stats the visual connection. Must-haves include the why you-your book; the benefits that readers will get when they buy it; what the moneys will be used for; AND a call to action.

    Videos can be fun, poignant, and even quirky. But you have to have one.

8   **Rewards are essential.**
    Make sure that they are relevant to the level that is being invested. Getting a book for

$100 won't fly—the supporter is looking for more. Liven them up—that's why you studied what other campaigns have done.

9 **Family and Friends are critical to your success.**
The majority of campaigns are seeded by family and friends (At least 30 percent of the total funding goal). So, don't be shy. You need their help and moneys.
Ask … and you may have to come back and ask again to throw you over the final hump at the end. That's when you usually have a "reward in your pocket to offer as an enticement" to those who supported you early-on.

10 **List Building is ongoing.**
Gather names and emails everywhere you go. Ask friends and family for names and emails of those within their circles who might be receptive if you sent an email sharing your launch with them when the big month arrives.

11 **Social Media is essential.**
Your Tweets, Facebook postings, Blogs and other social media portals are elementary to your success. You need to be building

your numbers. Not just a few hundred—thousands. You will need the social media connections of colleagues and friends who will do shout outs on your behalf to their followers to support your campaign.

12 Create a Call to Action.

If you don't do this in your written material, your video and in person—people don't hear your message. A Call to Action is critical to your success.

How to Create a Crowdfunding Campaign for Authors and Writers was designed to be short, informative, and a how-to for your success.

Did it work for you?

We authors depend on your shoutouts that come via reviews. Would you take a few minutes and post a review on Amazon for me?

Thank you.

Thanks to My Village

SOME BOOKS COME TO authors over what seems like an eternity of time; others come roaring in like a lion. *How to Create Crowdfunding Success for Authors and Writers* had to happen. In fact, it was long overdue.

Originally, this book bubbled up while I was teaching the *How to Write a Book in 4 Weeks* course in my hometown of Denver, Colorado—a course I now offer online as well. Leading and teaching the class, it made sense that I too would write a book and demonstrate in a hands-on approach that I could deliver what I preached. Initially, I had planned on 50 blunders and began to pull them together. The rewrites took a bit longer than I planned. It wasn't my priority, after all; I had clients' books to work on. Then I started tweaking. Of course, I would add a "goose" to each item I identified—a what to do next. The TIP. Then, I got the idea—what the heck, let's shoot for 100. My mini-book is bigger than the others in the *AuthorYOU Mini-Guide* series—you see, there was so much material in my years of book shepherding to pull from! You get 101 PLUS within the narratives and Tips—they total over 200!

I reached out to respected colleagues and publishing professionals for their sage advice and hiccups they routinely see: Helen Sedwick, Patti Thorn, Michele DeFlippo, Kelly Johnson, Phil Knight, Nick Zelinger, Joan Stewart, Joel Friedlander, Tom Campbell, Brian Jud, Bret Ridgway and Rebecca Finkel, and of course, my book shepherding clients. In many cases, they are the walking talking survivors of many blunders, bloopers and boo-boos.

In the late summer of 2015, my publishing comrade and long-time friend Dan Poynter and I had one of our hour plus phone calls sharing our "greatest hit blunders" ... many are threaded throughout. I miss him—as thousands of others do—with his passing.

As The Book Shepherd, at times, I am amused, alarmed and downright appalled at some of the repeated mistakes authors create themselves or allow themselves to get sucked into. This needed to be a book, not a huge one, but one that is not GeekSpeak or loaded with charts and graphs—a how-to book that is easy to understand and loaded with practical tips and guidance.

As with the other books in the *AuthorYOU Mini-Guide* series, the format had to say *fun*. You get a book with big solutions and ideas. To bring a small book to life, the team came together again in the first round of emails.

Thank you to the awesome Nick Zelinger of NZ Graphics. I can count the fingers on one hand to identify book and cover designers who are as flexible as Nick is. "Sure, why not, let's see what we can do this time with those sheepie guys of yours." Love what he continues to do.

Thank you to my other favorite cover and book designer Rebecca Finkel. When it was time for the "do over" of the series, her vision for the covers was perfecto!

Thank you to Leah Dasalla, who took my sheepie guys and made a series of posters and banners to flow throughout the book. "This has been a fun project. Are you going to do another one like it?" Yes I am—it's the next in the *AuthorYOU Mini-Guide* series.

Thank you to Kelly Johnson, my favorite Geek Girl, who can do just about anything behind the scenes ... and take center stage when need be. "I love those sheepie guys ... they always make me smile." As they do me.

Thank you to Don Sidle, the sheepie guy creator. Coming back for a fifth book appearance, the sheep family has had quite a journey. "I like whimsy and goofy—you inspired me to bring the sheep out!" Who would have thought that sheep would become part of my branding and who would have thought of adding a wheel chair, crutches and a boo-boo arm to the mix? Don did.

Thank you to my first line editor, John Maling, who does the tweaking in rewrites—"are you sure you really want to say it this way?" "This is much needed ... it's simple enough, limits the overwhelm and eliminates the unknown. I like it." Always helps when your editor "likes" the book!

Thank you to Peggie Ireland, my cold-eye editor who always catches things my eyes can no longer see and my head knows have already been fixed, and haven't been. "I love these practical, hands-on books." Me too—I think I know what the next one is ... then another pops up.

It takes a village to create a book. It takes a village to keep an author going. And it takes a village to be successful in your book publishing. I am blessed to have my awesome village. Find yours and take care of it.

Judith

Meet Judith Briles

The Book Shepherd

About the Author

MEET DR. JUDITH BRILES, known as The Book Shepherd, Author and Publishing Expert, Book Publishing and Crowdfunding Coach, Conference Speaker, Radio Host and the Founder and Chief Visionary Officer of *AuthorYOU.org*, a membership organization created for the author who wants to be seriously successful. She's been writing about and conducting workshops on publishing since the '80s and coordinates the annual *Publishing at Sea* working cruise conferences.

Judith is the author of 42 books—18 published with New York houses until she created Mile High Press in 2000. Based in Colorado, she's published in 17 countries and with more than a 1,000,000 copies sold of her work. *How to Create Snappy Sassy Salty Success for Authors and Writers* joined her multi-award winning bestseller, *Author YOU: Creating and Building Your Author and Book Platforms. Author YOU* was selected as a Book of the Year in the Writing|Publishing category at the IndieFab awards and is considered the must have workbook for Platform building.

How to Avoid Book Publishing Blunders is the third book in the *AuthorYOU Mini-Guide* series joining *How to Create Crowdfunding Success for Authors & Writers* and *The Authors Guide to AudioBook Creation* by Richard Rieman. *How to Create a Million Dollar Speech* and *The Author's Walk* are now members of her publishing family.

Judith has chaired numerous publishing conferences and is a frequent speaker at writer and publishing conferences. She knows publishing and she gets the challenges that authors go through in creating and publishing their books. Known as The Book Shepherd to many, she's personally guided hundreds of publishing clients throughout the United States, Canada, Mexico, Australia and Hong Kong.

Throughout the year, she presents her Judith Briles Unplugged events. Over two days, strategies and how-to are delivered for: Book Publishing, Book Marketing, Social Media, or Speaking.

All details are under the Experiences tab on her website.

Follow *@AuthorU* and *@MyBookShepherd* on Twitter and do a "Like" at AuthorYOU and Judith Briles-The Book Shepherd on Facebook. Join the AuthorYOU LinkedIn group and the Book Publishing with The Book Shepherd group on Facebook To book a consult with Judith, you can secure a 30-minute or 60-minute slot at: *https://TheBookShepherd.com/pick-judiths-brain/* or go to her website.

Since inception, authors have downloaded over 9 million episodes of AuthorU-Your Guide to Book Publishing podcast. Access it on iTunes at as well as through her website or at *http://bit.ly/BookPublishingPodcast*

Speaking and Book Shepherding are what Judith does. If you want to create a book that has no regrets or bring her to your conference, contact her at *Judith@Briles.com*.

© 2016 All rights reserved. Judith Briles, The Book Shepherd

Working with Judith

Judith Briles Consults and Speaks ...
Would You Like to Listen, Learn, Publish?

Judith Briles would be delighted to participate in your publishing conference or to speak to your group. For Book Shepherding and Book Consulting, email or call her offices. If you want a highly interactive, informative and fun presentation or workshop, call or email her for availability:

Judith Briles
JudithBriles.com
Judith@TheBookShepherd.com
www.TheBookShepherd.com
303-885-2207
Consulting by the Hour or by the Project

Workshops and Keynotes include: *Is There a Book in You?, CrowdFunding Your Book Project, Create Ninja Book Marketing, Avoid the Blunders that Can Sink Your Book, Boring Speeches Suck! ... Create a Talk that Sells Thousands of Books and Can Make Over a Million Dollars, Create Your*

Author and Book Platforms, Creating Confidence as an Author & Writer, If Publishing Is in Your Midst ... Which Option is for YOU and YOUR Book?, Stop the Social Media Insanity

You want information and resources to help you sell books. My blogs, radio shows that are available in podcasting format and social media accounts are right up your alley in supplying information for today's author. Let's get connected:

The Book Shepherd Daily
http://tinyurl.com/TBSDaily

Blog
TheBookShepherd.com website

http://bit.ly/BookPublishingPodcast

Radio - iTunes Podcast Feed
*http://toginet.com/rss/itunes/
AuthorUYourGuideToBookPublishing*

Instagram
Instagram.com/judith.thebookshepherd

Pinterest
JudithBriles

Twitter
@MyBookShepherd

LinkedIn
LinkedIn/in/judithbriles/

Facebook
Judith Briles

The Book Shepherd
facebook.com/TheBookShepherd

FB Group: Publishing with The Book Shepherd
facebook.com/groups/BookPublishingHelp

The AuthorYou Mini-Guide Series

How to Create Snappy Sassy Salty Success for Authors and Writers is the perfect pick-me-up for the aspiring author; for the author who has landed in a rut; or just a bit of inspiration.

How to Create a Million Dollar Speech delivers the secret sauce for book sales and turning an author's wisdom and expertise into the golden ticket.

How to Create Crowdfunding Success for Authors and Writers offers the latest up-to-date information on how successful crowdfunding campaigns can work for you.

How to Avoid Book Publishing Blunders gives you 101 gems of book publishing wisdom—essential reading for all authors wishing to self-publish.

New from Judith Briles:

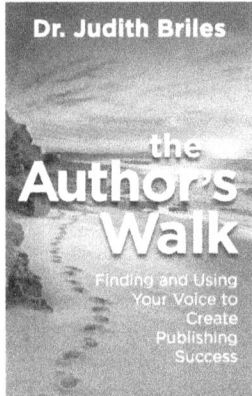

More inspiration and expert guidance from bestselling author and author advocate Judith Briles.

www.ingramcontent.com/pod-product-compliance
Lightning Source LLC
Chambersburg PA
CBHW071741080526
44588CB00013B/2119